Firstborn

FIRSTBORN

William Hulme

PUBLISHING HOUSE
ST. LOUIS   LONDON

Concordia Publishing House, St. Louis, Missouri
Concordia Publishing House Ltd., London, E. C. 1
Copyright © 1972 Concordia Publishing House
ISBN 0-570-06763-4

MANUFACTURED IN THE UNITED STATES OF AMERICA

CONTENTS

CHAPTER 1

A Time of Concern— and Confidence

So you are going to have a baby! I realize I am addressing both of you—husband and wife—and literally only the wife has the baby. Yet the husband in a sense is having it also. After all, you two have become one flesh, and if you had not, there would be no baby.

Your Little Scout

Not only are you having a baby—but your *first* one. Every first happening has a uniqueness all its own. Because he is your first child, your baby will lead you into many other *first* experiences. First of all he introduces you to the experience of being parents—which is something far more than giving birth. He will also be your first child to enter school. So he introduces you to the PTA. He will also be the first to enter adolescence and will introduce you—rather roughly, I predict—into what it means to be the parent of an adolescent.

He also may be the first of your children to marry, and this will thrust you into being in-laws. He may also duplicate your feat and have a baby, and you will discover yourself a grandparent. Therefore, we shall call this firstborn of yours the family scout, because he is out in front initiating you, as well as himself, into all kinds of new experiences.

Are you an oldest child? If so, you know something about this role from firsthand experience. If not, perhaps your spouse is. At any rate you occupied some distinctive position in the order of events in your previous family, and as a result you know why it is that no children in the same family have the same environment even if they have the same parents.

Perhaps you have noted that I refer to the baby as "he." Do you want a boy or a girl? How about your spouse? I suppose most of us are not too particular on the first one. The idea of having a baby seems more important than what kind. I say "he" simply because of a cultural tendency to use the masculine pronoun when we are speaking inclusively of both sexes—and also because I do not wish to refer to the baby as an "it."

A Great Event

Now that we are somewhat acquainted, let me offer you my congratulations. Whether you have waited long for this event or whether it came quickly, whether you "planned" for it or it did its own planning, you are fortunate. It is a great experience to partner with your mate in the rearing of your child—to be joined by another who is the product of you both. As God is the Creator and you are created in His image, so now by His power you participate in the process by which He creates new life. Your marital union is quite obviously a productive union.

There will soon be no other reason for having a baby than *wanting* a baby. In fact, the time may come when a couple will have to get permission from governmental authority to have a baby. The population explosion is upon us. The Biblical directive from the account of the creation, to be fruitful and multiply and fill the earth, has run its course. We have multiplied, and the earth is filled. Now the problem is overfilling. The advances in contraception make it possible for husband and wife to have sex relations at any time without conception. So, one by one, many of the former reasons for having children have become passé. But this provides opportunity for the Christian couple to seek the will of God more deeply than was often the case in the past.

There is no danger, however, that children will go out of style. There will always be takers simply because having a child is a joy in itself. It is like marriage. Many former reasons for marriage—economic, social, procreational—are less relevant today. Yet people will still choose to marry because it is a very satisfying arrangement for living for both men and women.

Concerns Behind the Joy

In spite of your justifiable joy in anticipating this "blessed event," I imagine you also have some concerns. It is a new experience, and you have some apprehensions over it. Will everything go well? You are living at a good time. In contrast to days gone by, the overwhelming majority of births go well for mother and baby. In other ages and even now in some other cultures, the ratio is not nearly so good—for all of which our own medical science deserves much of the credit.

Of course, this does not mean that all risk is eliminated. Some babies, for example, continue to be born with deficiencies of one sort or another. Again it is similar to what has happened in regard to marriage. There is far more help available today for marriage, both in premarital guidance and marital counseling, than in any other era. If people avail themselves of these opportunities, their chances for a good marriage are excellent. Even so, there is still the possibility of failure. Although you knew this, you still went ahead with your marriage. You had faith you were making the right decision. So also with having a baby.

Although your mother had you, and you know others who have had babies, the experience is new for *you*. With any *first time*, there is the element of the unknown—and this can be frightening. It is not unknown only to the wife, who has the experience of giving birth, but also to the husband, who has the experience of somehow, some way, standing by. So you need to be helpful to each other as you approach the event.

The wife is dependent on her husband's presence — his dependability. New fathers sometimes try to hide their uneasiness by appearing blasé, unconcerned, failing to realize how important they are in the whole affair. They seldom act this way the second time. While the wife is going through the pregnancy period, the labor pains, and the process of giving birth, she needs her husband.

The husband, on the other hand, needs his wife's confidence in him. His role is nebulous. The wife is apparently doing and enduring it all. He needs her to help him find his role. Rather, she actually gives it to him as she lets him know why and how and when she desires his presence, comfort, and support.

Confident Toward Parenting

As you look beyond the birth event itself to the actual task of being a parent to your child, I imagine you feel more confident. If you are like the rest of us, we seem to assume that we will do all right in this category. In fact, it is not uncommon to assume that you will do a better job of parenting than your own parents have done with you. These are "famous last words." If every generation had improved on their elders as they had anticipated, we would have reached utopia long ago. But we haven't. We seem more often to repeat the past than to improve on it.

Perhaps our confidence regarding our parenting is a bit naïve. How much actual preparation do most of us receive before we are plunged into the task by a birth? For what is probably the greatest challenge — parenting a child — there is the poorest of preparation. In contrast there is much preparation for marriage. The whole period of courtship and engagement is preparatory for living together. In fact, it is on the basis of this limited relationship that a couple decides whether to go on to the full commitment of marriage. If they decide to do so, the pastor will undoubtedly give them some premarital guidance before he performs the ceremony. Yet these preparations for marriage are limited in the amount of help they can give. You have to "get into it" before you can really understand what is involved. This is why some pastors are finding it profitable to meet with the couple three to six months after the wedding for a follow-up guidance session.

On the other hand, you really have been prepared for parenthood in one way or another. Actually, you have had twenty years of conditioning for the role in your own home, except you were the child rather than the parent. Human beings have the longest maturation experience—eighteen to twenty years of it compared to just two for an animal as big as the elephant. So you have had a long and impressionable time for parent-child patterns to take shape within you.

When you are emotionally worked up—and parents at times get this way—you will tend to reenact the behavior pattern you have witnessed under similar circumstances, only now you will be the parent instead of the child. You have probably noticed this tendency to reenact the old family patterns already in your marriage. Have you caught yourself at times feeling and acting toward your mate as your parent of the same sex did toward his or her mate under similar circumstances?

On Leaving the Old

In your wedding service something was said about leaving father and mother to cleave to your mate. But this is not easy to do. We tend to bring the old home into the new home in one way or another. Depending on how you feel toward your previous home, you may either try to duplicate with your child what your parents did in regard to you, or tend to disparage what you had as a child and to covet what you did not have (or at least you didn't think you had) for your child. In either case you would not have "left" father and mother, and would have certain predispositions that you need to examine. Otherwise, you may unconsciously force your agenda on your child.

It is one thing to appreciate one's previous home or to recognize honestly its shortcomings. It is another thing, however, to be so tied to this home that you either uncritically assume that everything about it was superior (especially to your mate's home) or just as uncritically desire to do everything in contrast to it. Such compulsive bias would leave your new role of parenthood at the mercy of your past hang-ups.

Instead, you will want to approach your new role as an expression of your *present* home. You and your spouse have formed a unique union, which ought to have every opportunity to profit from the past without being bound to it, either by adulation or rejection.

Looking Ahead Realistically

The parental joys you anticipate are like marital joys. They are mixed in with irritations and discouragements. This description is probably not too unlike what your own parents experienced with you. There were times, I am sure, that they worried about you or were depressed over their role as your parents. You probably did not know this at the time. Parents rarely tell their children when they feel they are failures as parents. You probably won't either.

There were also times undoubtedly when your parents thoroughly enjoyed you and were proud of you. You may not have known this either. Parents often fail to tell their children their good feelings toward them. We are usually freer in family living to express the negative than the positive. I hope you won't fall into this pattern with your child. There is one way you can work at preventing this even before the child is born. Practice on your mate. The way we treat our marital partner affects the way we treat our children.

CHAPTER 2

What Will Others Think!

The subject of this chapter could easily be presented in a frightening way. I do not wish to do this — not only because I do not wish to frighten you but also because your ability to profit from it depends on your being positive rather than negative toward the challenge presented. At the same time I do not want to minimize a very real problem. If you know my procedure, perhaps we can avoid both dangers. In the first part of the chapter I will present the picture as I see it. In the latter part I will talk about positive things you can do about it. If the first part tends to be depressing, you will know that help is on the way.

Pressure on the Oldest

Your baby will be your firstborn. By this simple fact your baby will be the recipient of more pressure than if he were the last born. Psychologists have listed the characteristics of oldest children that result from this pressure. I am not going to identify these characteristics. If I did and you did not consider them good characteristics, you would be concerned about developing their opposites in your child — and for the wrong reason. You may have already thought about some of these negative possibilities. They may be negative primarily because of the warped perceptions of our competitive society. We are overly concerned about the impression others are receiving of our child.

This concern begins early — even in the hospital. Many

of us have not seen a brand-new baby before we have our firstborn. We have little idea what to expect. When we first see the little creature, it may be a bit of a shock. He may not look at all as we had anticipated. Then there is the problem also of how he progresses. Is he getting enough food? Is he making the desired gains? All these are legitimate concerns. Yet the comparison of your baby with other babies has already begun.

We are accustomed to a competitive world and automatically transfer these attitudes toward any enterprise, including the production of children. Having a child, however, is not a competitive enterprise. It may be the first noncompetitive involvement you have experienced. Our society does not prepare us for such an experience. Consequently, we easily fall into the old patterns.

This competitive tension continues even more as the baby is able to get about. He is a highly visible little fellow. The competitive enterprise assumes an audience. The highly visible, highly audible baby is seen and heard by others. What will they think? Because the judgment of the audience is the key to competitive success, we are very sensitive to any indication of disapproval. When the child is on display, the parent is on edge. His anxious eye shifts with the movements of the child, and his overreacting hand is constantly curtailing the child's movements.

I know. I have done it myself. I have also witnessed it with others. When I have witnessed it, I have, of course, been a visitor. When I have done it, it was when I *had* visitors. The anxious parent is confused over the child's role. He finds it difficult to let the child be a child. The resultant tension diminishes the enjoyment of all concerned. The parent is taking the child's behavior *too* seriously. The visitor feels it; so undoubtedly does the child. Being overly anxious, our touch is heavy. In spite of our disdain for the word, we become coercive.

A Parent-Centered Problem

The problem I have described is parent centered rather than child centered or visitor centered. A new parent naturally feels awkward in the parental role. Despite our mental preparations, things rarely turn out precisely as anticipated. When problems arise, we are temporarily thrown for a loss. Normally these problems would resolve themselves. But they create a secondary problem — parental anxiety. This latter problem is worse than the first. Preoccupied with his concerns over the child, the anxious parent *over*reacts — putting more importance on the child than the child can tolerate. The parent is unsure of himself and shows it.

The old adage that children should be seen and not heard is happily passé. Children need also to be heard, to be listened to. The old adage, however, was not all wrong. Children are not adults. In the company of adults they are more comfortable with a peripheral role than a central one. In former days they made their bows and then were removed. In our day they tend to remain — and in the center of attention. They do so by being cute or by being naughty or by alternating between the two. Neither situation is good. Between the two extremes there is a happy medium.

Before the child can develop his own place as a child, this place must be developed in the parent's mind. The overconcern and awkardness that go with any new experience can scarcely be avoided in parenthood. The attempt to avoid them would create even more stiffness. A new parent is a new parent! But this is not the problem. These natural anxieties will easily resolve themselves in the learning process of both parent and child. In fact, you may do some things better as a parent *because* it is your first time. There are qualities of freshness that are wholesome and are never quite duplicated when the experience is repeated.

The cultural aggravation of our anxieties, however, *is* avoidable. It is to this problem that we should give our attention. It was bugging you long before you became an expectant parent, and its influence extends far beyond the parental role.

What Impression Do You Want to Make?

If we are to do something about the avoidable part of parental anxiety, we need to get something else straight in our minds besides the child's place. That something else is summed up in the familiar watchwords, "What will others think!" What would you like them to think? What do you want them to think about you? about you as a parent? about your child?

Why do you want others to have these specific impressions? What need would it fill if they did? How would you be threatened if they did not? Usually we are concerned less about people generally than about specific persons. Whose impressions are you primarily concerned about? Your parents'? Your spouse's parents'? Your brothers' and sisters'? Your friends'? Your neighbors'? Your fellow workers'? Not only is it natural to be concerned about others' opinions, it is good. How can we care about people if we do not care about their impressions? But caring is one thing, and dependence is another. When we are dependent on what others think for what we think, we give them too much power over us.

Perhaps you are one who says, "I couldn't care less what others think!" Is this what you want them to think—that you don't care what they think? I am really not trying to "pull your leg." People who pride themselves on their indifference to what others think are often just as concerned about making an impression—the "right" impression—as are people who care too much. It would trouble them if they thought people had the impression that they cared. In either case we have the same problem—the need to create a certain picture of ourselves in the minds of others.

The silly part of this concern about what others think is that these *others* are probably just as concerned about what *you* think. All of us seem to be caught in varying degrees in this rat race of making the *right* impression on others. It almost sounds like we are afraid we are not the sort of person we want others to think we are. Hence the anxiety about giving the "right" impression—whatever that may be. The result is an egocentric barrier to our relationships. Who can care about another person as a person when he is primarily concerned about the impression he is making?

There is a more satisfactory way of relating to people. We have to be secure in our own person, however, to achieve it. When we are anxious over what others think, we are automatically on the defensive. Instead of opening up, we close up. What then are we defending? There is nothing to prove. You don't have to produce the outstanding child. You are not competing with other parents. You will be fallible as a parent as you are fallible in every other way. You will make mistakes . . . be insensitive . . . lose your patience.

Obviously, if you insist on being a perfect parent, you will not only be disappointed but miserable. If you can accept your imperfection, you can learn to be content . . . to let others be . . . to let yourself be . . . to enjoy rather than defend. You will grow along with your child. These are not merely nice-sounding words. God has given us the power to do this through the Good News that He accepts us as we are. We don't have to defend ourselves before Him. He knows us even better than we know ourselves—

and still loves us. He loves not only our better self but our total self. If He can do it, we can learn to do it too.

The story is not completed in the beginning. There is mystery in every venture of life, including parenthood. Parents are something like theological professors. I happen to be both, and so I see the similarity. In theological education we are tempted to think that we are teaching the students everything they need to know so that they leave the seminary as finished products for the ministry. Actually what we are really doing is assisting them to be the kind of persons who can recognize enough of what is going on in any situation to have some idea of how to respond to it. From this point on, the new minister continues to learn — long after he has left the seminary.

The same goes for parenthood. Your child will learn also when he is away from you. He will learn also after he has left your home. Your task is to provide him a home base that will help him become the kind of person who can learn from his life situations. This is a learning process that begins in infancy and continues through old age.

When we see our role in this light, it is not only relaxing to us as parents but also to our child. When we are anxious that our child make a good impression, we give him powers that he should not have and does not want. He has the power to sabotage his parents by withholding the expression they desire. Now he controls them rather than vice versa. He can hurt and perhaps even destroy those on whom he is dependent. This is too much power for a child — it frightens him and also causes him unnecessary guilt.

Our intimate relationships are values in and of themselves. When we add other demands to them, the relationship becomes a bargaining type of exchange. You have something I want, I have something you want; so let's make a deal! When this occurs in intimate relationships, the feelings are too involved for such an exchange. Instead of exchanging our commodities, we withhold them as a means of retaliation. Those whom we love we at times also may hate. Children who are given this power learn quickly how to use it to the most effective advantage. Yet they suffer from it as much as the parents.

When the relationship is kept within the structure of an intimate relationship, what we each want from the other we already have. The child is loved for what he is, as he is, and not for his good behavior, cute sayings, intellectual skills, or performing talents.

We are important to our children, but we are not gods. We are not the decisive influence in our children's lives that our society would lead us to believe. Ours is not the power to mold and shape. The child is no "product." He is a person who contributes as well as receives. Created in God's image as were you, he enters into life *with* something. He picks up a lot more as he goes along—from you, from others—but always "under God." Your child is God's child. This has something to say about your role as a parent.

CHAPTER 3

A Child with God as His Father

The Meaning of Baptism

If you belong to a church that practices infant baptism, you will probably be thinking about this event soon after the baby's birth. Should you and your spouse reside in your home community, the new baby's baptism may be the time when the relatives have a family celebration. On the other hand you may be one of America's mobile society and live far away from your folks. Even so, one or more of the new grandparents may arrive for the event. You may also be thinking of specific relatives or friends as baptismal sponsors for your baby. Even if you will be alone, there are the pastor and the congregation in which the baptism will take place. They are your church family — or at least your potential church family. Baptism is a social event.

Perhaps you belong to a church that does not baptize infants. Instead you have a dedication rite. Infant dedication and infant baptism are not the same. Yet they have similarities. There is a difference in emphasis between being dedicated to the Lord and being received by Him into His family. The feelings of the parents, however, may be similar. In both there is the acknowledgment that God is the Father of the child. Since I follow the infant baptism tradition, I will discuss the significance of God as Father from this viewpoint.

When your child is baptized, he is received into the family of God. Perhaps you are wondering why he should not be in the family of God from the beginning. In one sense he is. God is his Creator. Yet the child needs also to be *received* into the family of God. He enters a world under judgment. In Christian terms it is a world "under the cross." Creation is in need of redemption. Your child participates in this human predicament by virtue of being a human being.

Even Jesus was baptized. He insisted on it, though John, His baptizer, was reluctant. "Let it be so now," Jesus said, "for thus it is fitting for us to fulfill all righteousness." As the pioneer and perfecter of our faith, He leads the way for us to follow. Those who are baptized are baptized *into* Christ—have *put on* Christ. God identifies us with Him. As St. Paul says, we are buried with Christ by baptism into death, that as Christ was raised from the dead, we also should walk in a newness of life. Being received into the family of God is a second birth. We die to the old—the corrupted creation—and are resurrected to a new creation.

It probably sounds fantastic to talk this way about a newborn child. What is there in such a child that could possibly need redeeming? There may be some who wince at the words *original sin,* but the fact is that most of us believe what the words mean. There is much potential in the baby that is not discerned or even developed for months or even years. One example would be teeth. Though the baby is toothless, he will develop teeth if given sufficient nourishment.

So also with sin. No one would dispute the sinfulness of our society. Few would question their own sinfulness. Where does it all come from? From the environment? It surely helps. But where did the environment come from? Society cannot exist without individuals. Society shapes persons, but it is also persons who shape society. Original sin is a complex aspect of our faith, but for the purposes of our discussion here let us agree that it includes the idea that every human being is predisposed to selfishness. Our social setting encourages it. Even your family life will do this. At the same time each of us responds to the setting. The potential is within us.

The Good News of Jesus is that God has overcome the barriers erected against Him by human selfishness. He is our Father in spite of the sinfulness of the human situation. Baptism is His way of making this clear to each individual. Jesus chose water — a necessity for human life with much symbolic significance — as the means for conveying His Good News. In baptism God receives the child into the society — the family — of the reconciled. This too is a necessity for human life. Your baby is being formed by the power of God to be born in the flesh and by the same power to be born also in the spirit.

God Works Through and Beyond Our Parenthood

As God has worked through you and your spouse in the creative process of bringing to birth, so also He will work through you in rearing the child to maturity. As the developing infant needs its mother's womb to mature to birth, the developing child needs the secure ties of loving adults to grow into adulthood. Consequently, the sponsors at the baby's baptism should be the parents as well as the godparents. Who other than the adults with whom the child lives can bring him up in the nurture and admonition of the Lord?

It is good to have other sponsors also to encourage and support the parents. I have always appreciated the ties with my two godmothers — one of whom is still living. A child profits from adult relationships other than his parents. But these others cannot replace parents as long as the parents are alive and functioning.

When the parents present their child for baptism and profess their belief in the Good News, they show that they also as parents are "under God." They too are "under authority." They may hinder as well as help in God's care of the child, but since their authority is subject to His, their blunders are also subject to Him. Since He alone is God, He is bigger than human blunders. It is possible for parents to take themselves too seriously, particularly in matters over which they feel guilty.

Though limited in its scope, the parental role points to that which is unlimited. It is through us—imperfect as we are—that our children receive their impression of God. His parenthood is known to them through ours, even though He functions beyond us as well as through us. As children grow older, their mental image of God undergoes adjustment and change, but their initial picture is given to them by their parents. Obviously God is most capable of working through imperfection.

Because God functions beyond us as well as through us, He works through what we as parents would never plan. As human beings we cannot assume that we have the mind of God. Believing in God is the opposite of believing that we are gods. What we see in any present moment may be only a portion of what is actually transpiring. When we are aware of this, we not only approach each present moment with a degree of humility but are open also to the larger vision that is provided by faith. We leave room for mystery.

When things seem to be going badly with their children, parents are tempted by their anxiety to believe that the negativity they see constitutes all there is to see. In other words, they cease temporarily to believe in God. Most of us tend to be too protective of our children. We protect them not only from threatening situations outside the home but from tensions also within it.

Yet these tensions are characteristic of human life. Because they contain the potential for pain and suffering, they also are potential for growth and development. Our children should be permitted to face and endure at least some of them.

Although God works through human parents in the exercise of His own parenthood, He does not transfer the qualities of omniscience and omnipotence. To put it, in distinctly human terms, He does not shrink from His own responsibilities because He has fellow workers. He will continue to be God — if for no other reason than that the qualities of *Godness* are not transferable. Whenever these qualities are claimed by human beings or ascribed to them, the effects are disastrous.

Normally we associate these idolatrous incidents with popular leaders or national rulers. They occur also in family relationships. Not only are parents tempted to play God, but family members tend to demand from one another what only God can give. Probably for this reason Jesus resorted to the shock effect of hyperbole to warn against such idolatry. "If anyone comes to Me and does not hate his own father and mother and wife and children and brothers and sisters, yes, and even his own life, he cannot be My disciple" (Luke 14:26). It is asking too much of any human being or any family relationship to take the place of God. Sooner or later the idol destroys the idolater, and the idolater destroys the idol.

It is precisely this potential to hurt and destroy that worries parents. It is the concern over having too much power — more power than a human being can tolerate. The fear is that we will use it — destructively.

Naturally parents can abuse their children. Their difference in size and strength makes this obvious. The comparatively small number of parents who physically abuse their children is becoming a societal concern. Such parents are sick individuals, and their children become scapegoats for their pathological hostility. These unfortunate children need to be removed from their parents for their own safety.

For most parents the fear of doing some permanent damage to their children is exaggerated. I once heard child psychologist Fritz Redl say that a parent can sin against his child some two hundred and eighty times and not do any lasting harm. Children are tougher than we think, and we are less powerful than we fear. Redl's two hundred and eighty times reminds one of Jesus' seventy times seven—the figure He gave to indicate how many times one should forgive another. Like Redl He did not intend that one should *count* the times. Rather, He meant *don't worry* about the number.

The similarity between the child psychologist and Jesus goes deeper than their use of numbers. The power to harm is dissipated by the power to forgive. Your potential as a parent does not depend on perfection—which you do not have—but on being reconciled with imperfection. The forgiveness we give to others—seventy times seven—is extended first to ourselves—seventy times seven. Through the Good News of Jesus we are emancipated from the frustration of an impossible responsibility. Our child has God as his Father—and so do we!

The Contagion of Relaxation

The realization of forgiveness brings with it a relaxation that is contagious. It relieves the parent of the anxiety of trying to be God. This parental relaxation provides an encouraging environment for the child. It is communicated very early through the mother's touch.

Harry Stack Sullivan has studied the effect of maternal anxiety on the infant. It is evident from his observations that the infant is very sensitive to the mother's ease or lack of it. Anxiety comes out of unsureness. The sureness that comes through faith in God is picked up by the infant through the sensitivity of touch.

There is a great deal of emphasis today on touch. In

sensitivity groups and other forms of corporate intimacy, touching more than talking has brought the experience of communion. We live in a very lonely age. People compete with one another rather than *know* one another. Commenting on how young people may hug and cry with one another when they suddenly discover they have broken through their barriers, Michael Novak says, "Many young people from 'good middle class homes' have never known the sense of community with another human being. They are 'uptight' about touching one another." *

The communication of affection and peace through touch forms an early basis for the child's security. Nor is it a form of communication that should cease with infancy. Throughout the child's development it is important that parents communicate by holding, touching, caressing, as well as by words. We shall pursue this point in a later chapter.

Trust in God as our Father is a constructive power in parenthood. As you experience this trust, you will see beyond the present moment to this same moment as it exists before God. Those who see without the dimension of trust see only what is visible to their "human eyes." When you have God in mind, you are aware also of mystery — of what you cannot see with your eyes. You see the present moment as a *part* rather than the *whole*.

The known is always couched in the unknown. You can expect what those without faith would not expect and anticipate what they would not anticipate. In moments of discouragement you have resources for encouragement that are not visible to the "naked eye." In moments of elation, this same realization helps you "keep your feet on the ground." God sees more than we do. The very awareness of this is an incentive to humility.

* *A Theology for Radical Politics* (New York: Herder and Herder, 1969), p. 103.

Being under authority helps one to *be* an authority. Whether you like it or not, being a parent is being an authority. Your child will be dependent on your exercising this authority. He may resist it, but he also needs it — and wants it. Perhaps you have some misgivings about authority. Maybe you have resisted the authority of your own parents. Maybe you don't feel much like a "parental authority."

Despite our problems over authority, being under God's authority provides the security we need to function as authorities ourselves. When we can be authoritative without playing God, we can combine authority with humility. The exercise of such authority is less likely to stimulate "authority problems" in children. What you have you can give. Being under authority yourself, you can provide a similar relationship for your child.

Since you will be an authority who is also under authority, you too can grow — grow in your exercise of authority.

Chapter 4

Going Through
What You Went Through

"I know one thing for sure. I don't want my children to have to grow up like I did!" The young father who said this to me was black. His own father did not live with his mother so that she could receive aid for dependent children. They were a family of twelve children in a two-room tenement. His mother could never sleep soundly because she had to guard her children each night from the rats.

I would agree that no child should grow up like this in a land as affluent as ours. I sincerely hope that yours is not a poverty like this. In spite of the extremeness of these conditions, however, the sentiments of this young father are shared by many parents who do not share his poverty.

Sparing the Child Our Ordeals

It is natural to want to spare our children the ordeals that we had as children. Where the ordeals were due to poverty, we want to provide the opposite. If the ordeals were emotional, we want to spare them these also. Usually as new parents we have a clear picture of how to do it. The idea is to do things differently — oppositely — from what was done to us as children or by us.

The misgivings we feel over our own past give rise to the assumption that we develop best when we have all the conveniences. This is an assumption that needs to be challenged. By what means did you develop into the person that you are? I am sure the hardships you endured had something to do with it. Your own picture of yourself may not be very high. Most of us tend to have a low self-image. Yet your mate obviously thought enough of you to marry you. You were obviously attractive to him or her.

Because of our tendency to want to spare our children from these ordeals, it is good that the child has God as his Father. In using life experiences as a teacher, God is supportive of His children without being overly protective. He allows us to be exposed to difficult situations as a learning process, but He does not abandon us to them. As with Moses of old, He assures us, "My presence will go with you."

There is a difference between protection and overprotection. A child may need to be protected by his parent from involvements that are too much for him. As a parent you will be sensitive to these situations. Overprotection on the other hand stems from the parent's need rather than the child's. The parent's anxiety is too high to permit the child to take normal, even necessary, risks.

Problem in an Affluent Society

The need of parents to spare their children their own ordeals is characteristic of a changing society. New opportunities have opened to many who formerly would have been conditioned to assume the same social and economic status as their parents. The opportunities are so widespread that ours is called an affluent society. Not all share in this affluence. The *Other America* of which Michael Harrington wrote are the victims of poverty. Yet even these persons see affluence all about them, and particularly the young — like the father previously mentioned — have hopes of participating in it.

Ours is a day when luxuries are considered necessities and necessities are determined by what others have. A child being reared in this kind of society is likely to receive much but to be asked to contribute little. Because his parents want him to share these advantages that they lacked, he may be given so much that his initiative is inhibited. With the emphasis on his own satisfaction he may become insensitive to the needs and feelings of others. The usual result of such one-sided rearing is a child who is long on demanding and short on empathy—who is bored because he has not known the pain or the joy of "working out his own salvation."

Because a parent may not want his child to lack what other children have—particularly what the parent did not have—his child may lack the advantage of self-respect. This asset comes from contributing as well as receiving. Today we are witnessing the startling spectacle of middle-class young people envying and even emulating the poor. The advantages they have received—what their parents believed was so important—are seen by these youth as disadvantages.

Have you not caught yourself feeling inwardly proud when you talk about how rough you had it when you were growing up? The pride is in having made it on your own. In your desire to *do* for your child, watch that you do not deprive him of this same satisfaction.

Obstacles Are Built In

This does not mean that we have to provide obstacles for children to prevent them from having it too easy. There will be plenty of these without parental intervention. Life is a good teacher and has its own built-in character developer. What parents provide is the supportive relationship that encourages the child as he confronts these obstacles. Like God the Father, they offer the child their presence. Their relationship forms the base from which the child responds to life's challenges rather than evades them or is crushed by them. Although God promised to accompany

31

him with His presence, Moses still had to lead His people. God's presence provided him the confidence, the courage, to do it. It supported him during the many crises he faced during his leadership.

The confidence that parents who believe in God impart to their child is obviously characterized by this faith. It is the confidence that with faith in God and intelligent effort, obstacles can be surmounted. Things can change and change for the better. Faith provides the incentive for effort. When obstacles seem insurmountable and our confidence in our abilities is low, God is still able. Knowing this is an incentive to carry on. Our faith also helps us to *hold* on when the tendency would be to give up. God is not only able; He is also trustworthy. To *wait* on Him is to believe this.

How can you impart this attitude toward life's challenges to your child? Naturally you can use words—once he understands them. Yet he learns a lot before he learns words. Also words by themselves can be quite empty. The saying today is to put your body where your mouth is. How do you as a prospective parent meet your obstacles? If you are like a good many of us, you meet them sometimes with confidence and at other times with discouragement. Perhaps we cannot ask more of your child. Yet the fact that you do at times exercise your faith—that on occasion you act with courage—will be perceived. Children are sensitive to parental attitudes. Then when you use words or other symbols of communication to stimulate courage, your child will understand.

Stimulating Initiative

While children contribute to the atmosphere of the home, parents play the larger role at least initially. You will want to make available to your child the opportunities that stimulate his initiative. You will want also to provide the encouragement he needs to develop his own discipline. In these ways he discovers and develops his talents. You help him become what he is — or can be. Children need confidence in themselves to carry through in their pursuits. They can be taught to persist in spite of difficulties. Both the end product and the effort behind it should be praised.

Most of us are more prone to criticize than to commend. Yet we know that commendation is much more likely to produce incentive. Why then do we perpetuate these inefficient and self-defeating methods — especially in the family? Probably because we use our family members as scapegoats for our irritations and frustrations in general. Thanks be to God, we do not *have* to continue in the old ruts. We can *grow* in wisdom.

When your child shows initiative, it is important that you allow him to retain it. Let it be the child's pursuit rather than yours. The tendency is for the overly zealous parent to take over. We are so pleased that our child has an interest, a project, that we become too helpful, too suggestive. We give more than what is asked. This eager involvement of the parent detracts from the child's own initiative.

Take a father, for example, who delights in making things with his boy. When the father notices the child trying to build something, he moves in to help. Soon he is directing the project. The boy is learning how to do it better, but it is no longer "his thing." The father has taken over, and the boy's initial enthusiasm is gone.

This pattern may continue even to the choosing of a vocation. As he prepares for college, the boy decides on a profession. The father is overjoyed. He knows the right people to see, the best college to attend. He brags about the boy's choice to others. Soon the boy begins to experience a lag in interest. He thought it was his idea. Now it seems more like his father's again. His initiative has been usurped.

The only way such a boy can know whether his idea is

really his is for his father to stay out of it. Advice has been defined as that which every one wants to give but no one wants to receive. This is especially true of parental advice. It is most appreciated when it is requested. Not only do children need to do their own thing, they need also to retain the initiative for doing it.

As I finished writing the above sentence, my teen-age son entered the house to change his clothes. "I have to push my car," he said. "Do you want some help?" I asked. "I usually can get it started myself," he answered. My natural tendency was to disregard his resistance and go out to help him. However I recalled what I had just written, and so I said, "Okay." After a moment of silence he said, "You can look out of the window in a few minutes, and if I'm still there, come on out." He got it started himself.

Children are most likely to develop initiative and carry-through when these are traits in the family life pattern. Although you will be a parent, it is to be hoped that you will have other interests and pursuits as well. Your attitudes toward these other ventures also become part of the family atmosphere. It is easier for the child to adapt to the structure you provide for his development if he sees some correspondence to it in the way others in the family are living. When you insist on a certain specific behavior that he recognizes as a family pattern of behavior, you are confronting the child with reality.

When there is a discrepancy between the patterns of family living and what the child is asked to do, the parent often resorts to haranguing the child. When we harangue, we anticipate resistance. In fact we subconsciously encourage it. If there were no resistance, we would be startled. Haranguing is resisted by the child because it is interpreted as an infringement on his freedom rather than as a confrontation with reality. Although discipline and criticism are needed in the rearing of any child, it is the mark of wisdom not to rely on them for the child's development. For this we need the more positive approaches of encouragement and commendation.

CHAPTER 5

Your Child Will Be Unique

The child being formed in its mother's body is a duplicate of no other. Identical twins may seem to be duplicates, coming from the same conception. Often they look so much alike that only those who know them intimately can tell them apart. Yet as persons they are different, often quite different. Parents with several children are usually impressed by the differentness of each child — from infancy on. Your child will enter into life as a unique being.

In the current debates over revising the state abortion laws, there is a great deal of divergence over when the fetus becomes a person. In Roman Catholic circles the question is concerned with when the soul enters the body. Does the child become a person when he is born? at the earliest point in his development when he could survive a premature birth? at conception?

In the abortion quarrel these are moral and legal questions concerning the taking of human life. For our interest they are questions pertaining to the child's uniqueness. Whenever we speak of a person, we are speaking of uniqueness. Have you had the experience of meeting someone who reminded you of someone else? The fact that you are unusually impressed when this happens indicates that it does not happen often. Also the better you know this "similar" person, the more you become aware of his differences.

Where does this uniqueness come from? The most

logical explanation is heredity. Among the fantastic number of combinations that are possible from the mother's and father's genes, one such combination occurs at each conception. While the science of genetics can account for a great deal regarding physical and mental characteristics, the inheritance of personality traits is not so clearly defined. There is still much we do not know.

Our Anticipatory Images

I imagine you have some idea, picture, anticipation, of what your child will be like. This picture develops through the years from our various experiences, usually with children. When my wife and I were first married, we lived in with another family. There were several children in the family, one of whom was in her cute stage. I took a fancy to this child and, without fully realizing it, anticipated my own children most happily when I envisioned them in her image.

Before you met your mate, you had a mental picture also of what you anticipated. The old song made it quite specific. "I want a girl just like the girl that married dear old Dad." Besides this image of a parent, the stories we read, the movies we see, the new marriages of which we are aware—all may contribute to what we anticipate. This preconceived picture probably influenced your selection of your mate. We often find what we are looking for and are attracted to what we anticipate.

Yet this mental picture of your mate has had its subsequent tensions with reality. No person, even the one we select, is a carbon copy of our anticipations. Only in fantasy is this possible. Some of your misunderstandings with your mate may have been due to this divergence of the real person from the anticipated image.

If this divergence occurs even when the selective powers are in effect, how much more is it likely to occur with your child when your preconceived image has no selective power. You do not "choose" him any more than he "chooses" you. Your idea of what your child will be like will be confronted by the reality of who he is.

Despite its lack of selective power, it is helpful to take a look at your anticipatory image of the child. What are its characteristics? What values do these characteristics reflect — and why?

Our Cultural Values

The characteristics we value are not always those we supposedly revere. We are children of our culture and tend to value what our culture values. At the same time our religion may confront us with other values — even opposing values. A mother with a physically deformed child expressed her concern that our culture expects that all children will be born perfect. If they have visible defects, they are met with misgivings or even rejection. Our culture favors such characteristics for children as that they be cute, extroverted, and aggressive. It is only secondarily concerned that they be kind, considerate, and reflective. It is decidedly against their being shy, introverted, and compliant. But our religious values have tended to elevate kindness over aggressiveness and to find virtue in introversion as well as extroversion.

The parent who is caught in the bind between his culture and his religion may give double signals to his child. He says, "Be considerate," but he means, "Don't let anyone take advantage of you." He says, "Be yourself," but he means, "Don't lose your standing in the group." While double signals can initially confuse a child, he soon learns to play the game. He gets the message! Attitudes speak louder than words.

Although the new parent's mental picture of his child has no selective power, he may still try to manipulate the child to fit the picture. Though consciously unaware of what he is doing, he may reward the child when he fits the image and rebuff him when he does not. The child then learns what he must do to please the parent — conform to the image. By the same token he learns how to attack the parent — rebel against the image. While it is natural for a child to want to please his parents, it is also natural to deprive them of this satisfaction. Parental manipulation to fulfill an image puts pressure on the child to play a role or to sabotage it. The choice is between conformity or rebellion, and in neither will he be who he really is. The identity crisis we hear about today has one of its causes in this early pressure to play a role.

This problem is less likely to occur if you and your mate face openly, consciously, what your anticipations are, how they differ from each other, and to what lengths you may be inclined to go to pressure the child into fulfilling them.

Resistance to Difference

The alternative to pressuring the child to fulfill your image is to let the child communicate to you — tell you — who he is. This means that you will be open to recognize and appreciate his uniqueness. He will be a *new* person, unlike any other. The more we know people, the more we recognize these differences. Only those who are different from us, with whose grouping we are unfamiliar, seem alike to us. If you are a white person, you may appreciate a current joke. The black man was asked by the police if he could identify the person who robbed him. "No," he said. "All white people look alike to me."

Not only do those different from us all look alike to us, they even all seem to act alike. We put them all in the same image — usually negative. Yet in our own group — white, black, Oriental — we are highly sensitive to variations and differences in appearance and behavior. Obviously in this latter instance we are perceiving more accurately. The closer we are to people, the better we know them—know their uniqueness.

Snow crystals also all look alike, until we see them through a microscope. They are similar in this respect to human fingerprints. The fact that your child's fingerprints will be different from any other person's will be a means of identifying him. Many a thrilling detective story and actual police cases have climaxed in the identification of the criminal by the stray fingerprint he left behind. The fingerprint is a symbol of the uniqueness of the person who possesses it.

One of the saddest features of human history is the continuous failure of human beings to accept differences among themselves. Whether the conflict is between Jews and Gentiles, the English and the Irish, or the hill people and the gully people, the irrational resistance to difference is the same. The situation is sad, because differences are potentially enriching. Those who shut out others because they are different are themselves impoverished by the exclusion.

One of the most glaring examples of this resistance to difference is our own tragic racial situation. White people have been impoverished by their refusal to accept black people as their peers. Black people have been impoverished because they have received the white man's patronage rather than his fellowship. Only as each can accept the others as equal in their *differences* can either receive what the others have to offer.

The same problem of difference exists between male and female, particularly as they unite in marriage. They could not unite to form a marriage if they were not different. Yet these very differences cause trouble in many marriages. Men tend to look at things—sex, for example— differently than women. Instead of seeing these divergences as enhancing their life together, both husbands and wives have been known to resent the other because of these differences.

So also within these differences between the races or between the sexes, there are differences between the individuals in the same grouping. Here we encounter the same problem. The differences between individuals are also potentially enriching but are usually resisted instead. They become stumbling blocks to our accepting one another as persons. Yet if there were no individual differences, there would be no *persons*. Instead of allowing persons to be different, we try to screen out differences and enforce sameness. We have an image in our mind to which the person should conform — an image based on other individuals. We want duplication rather than uniqueness.

Children who enter the family encounter the same hazards to uniqueness from father and mother. The firstborn is the one most likely to get the "treatment." The molding process is often set — ready to go — by new parents eager to produce the ideal child. Ideal, however, means our *image* of ideal, which is patterned after someone else. *Ideal* is a comparative word. It implies standards of evaluating — something quite foreign to uniqueness. What the child is prepared to contribute by virtue of being a person is thwarted by the conforming pressures of comparison-conscious parents.

Since I am sure you do not wish this to happen, you can begin now to condition your mind to accept difference. Once you do this, you will discover yourself *appreciating* difference. Try it with your friends. Try it also with those who are not your friends but who possibly could be if you could accept their differences. Try it especially with your mate. It may help him — her — reciprocate by appreciating *your* uniqueness.

Spontaneity in Personal Relationships

When your child is born, he will add another person to your home. He will change it from marriage to marriage-and-family. You and your mate will develop your own relationship with him, and this in turn will have its effect on your relationship with each other. Personal relationships depend on persons interacting with each other. The differences in each person provide the stimuli for these relationships. So also with your relationship with your child.

The more genuine the personal relationship, the more the communication is spontaneous rather than calculated. Communication that is calculated stems from a defensive or protective posture. Concerned about how we will be received, we are cautious about what we say. Nothing is permitted to come out spontaneously lest we make the wrong impression. Calculated communication is motivated by the fear of being judged. We want instead to be rewarded. So we say what we sense the other wants to hear — or likes to hear.

Spontaneous communication, on the other hand, is based on our trust that we are accepted. Only in spontaneous communication can a person's uniqueness really be known. Otherwise it is partially hidden behind the calculated attempts to give an impression. While comparisons between persons are quite limited and peripheral, they nevertheless are potent influences for concealing the incomparable — personal uniqueness.

Obviously not all communication can be or should be spontaneous. All of us need controls and limits. When we can impose them ourselves, we are showing our maturity. Children need help from their parents to impose these limits. With some people — and at certain times — it makes sense to calculate what we say. If we are unsure of our acceptance or of the situation, wisdom is the better part of valor.

If there is anywhere that spontaneous communication should be possible, it is in the home. When one is loved unconditionally, he knows he is accepted — as he is. When our uniqueness is respected, we can be genuine in our relationships. As you respect your child's uniqueness, he will be encouraged to know who he is. He will share his identity with you — to the enrichment of your life and the life of your family. The family scout can do a better job of blazing the trail if he is first permitted to be who he is.

CHAPTER 6

Your Child Will Have a Body

First Medium of Communication

We adults depend excessively upon words for communication. One of the frustrating things about traveling in a foreign land is the inability to communicate with the people. We resort to all sorts of hand signs and facial expressions. The new arrival will not speak your language either. He will have a voice and will use it to inform you of his needs. You will have to investigate to see what he wants.

One thing for which he will ask — among others — is you. He wants to know you are there — to *feel* your presence, literally. His eyes may not yet be focused, but his sense of touch is functioning. Your first medium of communication with your child is through body contact. It is the entrance to his person.

Actually this medium of communication is no different in principle than the usual forms of communication. We adults depend largely on the sense of sight and hearing for communication, and the baby depends largely on the sense of touch. He soon learns also to distinguish voice sounds that go with affection — the lullaby for example. We communicate through our physical senses. Our body is the medium through which we interact with our environment and the people in it.

Your baby will notice other persons — including you — largely through his sense of touch. He will pick up your attitudes and your emotions in the way he "feels" your presence—your body. Your attitude toward his body communicates your attitude toward him. He needs your touch, your physical communication of affection, to feel secure in his new world.

Although we are learning more about its psychosomatic complications, the womb is a relatively secure environment. In contrast to its physiological consistency, the new environment depends on the response of other persons. The baby needs the assurance that his new universe is dependable. This assurance comes through specific physical satisfactions. Basic, of course, is regular feeding together with the pleasant sensation of sucking. Yet he needs more. Toys used to be made to hold the bottle so that the mother did not need to hold the child. All that is past. Children need food to survive, but they also need love. Babies who were not held while being fed did not prosper. Feeding from the mother's breast keeps the child in contact with the mother's body. Babies fed from bottles need this same contact. It is the means for communicating love—the human assurance of security. The body is not apart from the self but is the self's tangible expression.

First Medium of Education

The sense of touch is the first medium of education. Body contact between parent and child initiates the child's perception of sex. Sex education obviously begins early. It begins when the child reaches out for warmth and comfort from another person, and the person responds with affection. It begins when this person is acceptive also toward the child's bodily functions. While the odors associated with elimination are unpleasant, the process itself is both natural and satisfying. The proximity of the eliminatory and sexual areas makes for a ready transfer of attitudes.

Your baby will be a *sexual* person. Very early he will begin to show his maleness or her femaleness. He will be interested in his body—especially in his genitals and sexually sensitive areas. In his exploration he will not be concerned about the proprieties. Like Adam and Eve before the Fall he will be unashamed of his nakedness. He will attempt to satisfy his curiosity also with other children. When you "discover" him, he will be too innocent to be embarrassed.

Such unabashed curiosity and interest in things sexual is natural to his growing sense of identity as a person with a body. Lacking adult "modesty" regarding his sexual explorations as with his eliminatory functions, he needs parental direction. Direction, however, is not repression. The difference between them is important also when the child grows into puberty. His sexual desires need control—but not denial. Your "light touch" with his sexual curiosity will prevent him from becoming guilty over being a sexual person. It will assist him to accept his sexual nature as good.

Broadly speaking, sex is the affectionate outreach of one person to another. Sex education, therefore, centers in how we treat each other as persons. In infancy this is primarily communicated by how we treat each other's body.

Body contact teaches the child also about God. His religious education begins with his sense of touch. To put it in concrete terms, the diaper change tells the baby something about God. As you accept his eliminatory processes, you are accepting all of him. The diaper change is a major way of communicating this acceptance in the midst of what could be unacceptable—the soiling and odor. The security that the child experiences through physical affection assures him that the universe is friendly. It is *for* him rather than *against* him.

The use of words in religious education grows out of the nonverbal communication that teaches the fundamentals prior to the more formal, verbal religious training.

Nonverbal communication continues as a healthy supplement to verbal communication throughout life. When the verbal and the nonverbal clash instead of coincide, the nonverbal tends to have more validity than the verbal. In other words, our actions and attitudes speak louder than our words.

The child's first impression of God is his impression of his parents. As with family ties, religion is essentially a relationship. God is "God the Father almighty." Yet children think of their parents also as almighty. Their parental relationships, consequently, are basic to their understanding of God.

This transfer of parents to God in the child's mind led Sigmund Freud to conclude that religion was simply a projection of the father image into the universe. Some people do not feel mature enough to enter into adulthood without a parent, and so they conceive of a Heavenly Parent. There is enough truth to his observation to be disquieting. Our mental image of God may be highly influenced by the image we have of our parents. Though God is like a parent, however, He is not by this fact a human creation. Our image of Him is always something other —something less—than God Himself. Though we are dependent on human analogies for our picture of God, they can only approximate what He is like.

You may feel rather inadequate about being your child's first impression of God. You should! You are not God. No matter how good a job you do, you are limited by your own shortcomings. This is why we look to Jesus. He is the human expression of what God is like. St. John calls Him the Word who became flesh and dwelt among us. St. Paul calls Him the image of the invisible God. God has not abandoned us to the projection of parental images. He has made Himself known to us in Jesus.

Your child will not be confined to your relationship for

his knowledge of God. It is to be hoped that he will be involved in the larger family of God — the church — and in the church's means of grace — the Word and Sacraments. Here he will find resources that will enable him to see through you to Jesus. Still, you and your mate will be the child's first teachers of religion. Though your relationship to the child is naturally limited as a means for revealing God, it is still a most important influence for the establishment of his religious identity.

First Means of Achieving Identity

Body contact is again the first means the child has of achieving this identity. Love communicates self-worth. Its absence communicates the opposite. The Good News of Jesus confirms our worth because it is the assurance that God loves us. This Good News is initially communicated to the child through body contact. By this means relationships are initiated with the child on which he can depend. As he experiences your relationship as trustworthy, he has the basis for trusting in God. As he learns that he can count on your relationship, he has the security needed for his own development. Although we spend our entire life in learning to know ourselves, the process begins in the bodily contact of infancy. Before we can know ourselves, we need to be convinced that we are *worth* knowing. Whatever contributes to the child's sense of self-worth contributes also to his growing capacity to know himself.

Your child's education will begin in his preschool years. You and your mate are his first teachers. From you and your home environment he receives his first religious education, sexual education, and social education. Your family atmosphere is the first milieu other than the womb to represent the kind of universe into which he has entered. Your home will be his first church; your parenthood will be your basic church work.

Your church is dependent on you and your home. Its life and mission is not confined to what goes on within its walls. The church is a fellowship that exists wherever its people are involved with other people. Its program of Christian education centers in the home, beginning afresh with each new life. The fact that your child will have a body sensitive to human touch provides you with a medium of communication in these important years.

Communication Medium Also in Marriage

Body contact as a means of communication is not confined to children. It is important also to your distinctly adult relationship of marriage. While you would no longer get any pleasure out of sucking on a bottle, you enjoy the oral stimulation of kissing. As with the baby, however, you are not primarily concerned with physical stimulation for physical stimulation's sake. Rather you enjoy the stimulation as it involves you with another *person*. Bodily contact in sexual stimulation is an expression of personal intimacy. The tangible experience of touch—warmth, sensual pleasure—is a medium of communication for the spiritual outreach of one person to another—of love.

In your marriage sex has a religious significance. It expresses your relationship with your mate in a way that involves your total person—body, mind, spirit. According to the words of your wedding ceremony, you together have become "one flesh." In the union of bodies in sexual intercourse this intimacy is tangibly expressed. By mediating a personal relationship, sex is a way of knowing another. In the Bible the word used to describe sexual intimacy is *knowing*. The physical pleasure of pleasant sensation is joined with the spiritual pleasure of knowing your mate. On such an occasion your baby was conceived. *Knowing* in that instance was creative of new life.

Your firstborn will fulfill one of the basic purposes of

marriage—procreation. Procreation, however, is dependent on the other basic purpose—companionship. The birth of a child is dependent on people to care for him. As a totally helpless creature the child needs parents. He is dependent for his security on their living together. Significantly, those who *know* each other as mates may also desire to have a child together. When your child was conceived, the sexual function indigenous to each of these purposes coincided.

The importance of body contact in marital communication is much broader than sexual intercourse. The affectionate touch is appreciated by adults as well as by children. Mates need the reassurance that they are loved also. Sexual intercourse will be more satisfying if you and your mate are affectionate at other times as well. Physical affection enhances your sense of worth as well as your child's. It provides you with the satisfying feeling of intimate security. You *know* each other. This is the "environment"—the security—into which God will place your family scout. The love between you and your mate will be an assist to his development.

Chapter 7

Your Own Inner Child

The "Child" Continues in Adulthood

The similarity between adults and children in their sensitivity to body contact is not an isolated instance. The needs of adults and children are generally similar because we remain children even as we become adults. The early childhood image of ourselves stays with us, and the child that we were continues to express himself through it. This does not mean that our adulthood is something less than adulthood or that our development has been arrested. Rather it means that the adult does not exist apart from the child. This is not to be lamented. We need the child for personality balance. The child has the playful and light touch without which adult life would be impoverished.

Psychologist H. W. Misseldine calls this "child" the "inner child of the past." He sees each adult as really two persons—the adult that he is and the inner child of his past who breaks through the adult exterior from time to time. Misseldine sees your marriage, therefore, as a marriage of four rather than two persons—you and your mate as adults, and you and your mate's inner child of the past. Since marriage is an adult relationship, the inner children of the mates can produce crises as well as fun when they take over. As they get between the two adults, they change things to a child level of relating.

How your inner child behaves depends a great deal on your attitude toward him—how you picture yourself when you were a child. This mental image is usually shaped by how you perceived your parents felt about you. There may well be a difference between your parents' actual image of you and the image you thought they had. They may be surprised, even shocked, if you told how it seemed to you. They may perceive their attitudes much differently. You will have to face this same potential discrepancy in your relationship with your firstborn. He may not see you as you see yourself. Who then is right? Parents or children? Who knows?

Two things stand out, however. Even though they differ, parents and children are both telling it as they see it. Though the child may be wrong, the impression he has of his parents' image of him—right or wrong—affects his own image of himself. His impression is *real,* regardless of whether it is *true.*

According to Misseldine, growing up means becoming one's own parent of his inner child of the past. If the child is the child of the *past,* the person is an adult chronologically. Whether he is emotionally an adult depends on whether he has developed his own parental relationship with his inner child. If he still views this child of the past as he perceived his parents did, he is retaining his parents within him. He is still a child—their child. Though he be far from the parental home, he has not left father and mother. Yet it is as we *leave* father and mother that we can *cleave* to a mate. Marriage is an adult relationship, even though the inner child of the past is also involved. It is a help to any marriage if the mates are at least on the way toward becoming adults emotionally.

This difference between the child and the adult constitutes a gradual development. With the turbulent adolescent period in between, the difference involves the process of growing up. In contrast to physical growth, however, our emotional development can hit a snag, so that maturation is hindered. When this happens, it is often because the person in question cannot accept his own inner child. Since rejected children are rarely cooperative children, the inner child of the past may take over when the person should be in the adult role. In other words his inner child does not behave!

Transactional analyst Eric Berne has a variation of this same theme. Like Misseldine, he sees a parent and child within each person and joins them with an adult. Also like Misseldine he considers these "ego states" as personal and unique—the child is the child I was and am, the parent is the parent I had and still have, and the adult is the specific adult that I am and can be. We need all three—parent, adult, and child—for the needed personality balance.

Each, however, has his particular times to be dominant over the others. The situation in which the person is involved should determine which ego-state should dominate rather than his own compulsive or impulsive nature. Like Misseldine, Berne believes that when our child image is unaccepted, our child is most likely to act impulsively and create "behavior problems."

From Inner Child to Firstborn

The way in which we treat our inner child affects our parental role with our own children. In Misseldine's imagery, becoming our own parent to our inner child prepares us to be parents to our own children. Like mating, being a parent is an adult function.

As an example of how your approach to your inner child may affect your approach to your firstborn, take the matter of motivating behavior. A parent can inspire or defeat a child by the way in which he disciplines. When you do something of which you disapprove, when you fail to live up to your own expectations, do you berate yourself as a person or do you concentrate instead on ways and means of improving your behavior—performance—in the future? If you concentrate on berating yourself, you know from experience that you produce more misery than improvement. The biggest effect is the drain on your self-confidence.

On the other hand, if you concentrate on improving your behavior, you obviously believe you can do it. You have hope. This elevates rather than lowers your self-image. When you feel guilty over your failures, do you feel defeated, or do you feel determined to do things differently the next time? When you have become your own parent to your inner child, you guide him in ways that give confidence and hope.

So also with your firstborn. He will need plenty of parental guidance; children always do, including your inner child of the past. You will need to curb your firstborn's behavior for his own sake, but this is different from attacking his self-worth. He will need to be positively reinforced in his acceptable behavior and firmly checked in his unacceptable behavior. This is how he learns to discipline himself, to live in tune with reality. Basic to whether he can do it is whether he *believes* he can do it. This hope comes out of the conviction of self-worth—a healthy self-image—rather than its opposite. As you give this kind of reality guidance to yourself, your inner child, you can give it to another, your firstborn.

Where It All Begins

This ready transfer from the way you treat your inner child to the way you treat your firstborn shows how indiscriminate love is. Only a distortion of love—a conditional love (which is a contradiction in terms)—can be given to one person and not to another. Herein is the significance of the commandment "Thou shalt love thy neighbor as thyself." Our attitude toward ourself has a direct bearing on our attitude toward others. That which determines our attitude toward ourself is the image we have of our inner child of the past. This is the image we tend to project onto others, particularly onto our own children.

The commandment to love one's neighbor as oneself is coupled with another commandment: "Love the Lord thy God with all thy heart." The two are usually given together in the Bible as the sum of all commandments because they are interdependent. Love for God, love for neighbor, and love for self are all tied up together. St. John says that anyone who says he loves God and hates his neighbor is a liar. If he cannot love a neighbor whom he has seen, how can he love God, whom he has not seen?

If love of neighbor is dependent on love of self and love of neighbor is connected also with love of God, where does it all begin? The answer is the Good News. We love, says St. John, because God first loved us. He initiated the love sequence by sending His only begotten Son into our human situation to do for us what we could not do for ourselves. Since we cannot give what we have not received, God gave His love to us so that we also can give.

Our bondage to self-rejection is not easily broken. God's love must come through sacrifice and suffering. The breakthrough is in the cross of Christ. Through His broken body and shed blood there is reconciling power. The immediate application of His reconciliation is to our inner child of the past. The Good News is that this ornery, rejected, guilt-ridden image we carry about is a distortion. God loves you, your inner child. You are encouraged by God's own demonstration of love to love your own inner child.

Your inner child needs direction and not rejection, love and not indulgence, discipline and not beratement. He becomes lovable because he is loved rather than being loved because he is lovable. God's initiating love (called grace) initiates a personality revolution. So long as we have to be lovable—or *think* we have to be lovable—before we can be loved, we are doomed to unlovableness. But if you are loved as you are—if your inner child is loved as he is (which means even when he is unlovable)—the bondage is broken. He is emancipated from the hold of a negative self-image. The power comes from the experience of being loved as one is, as a unique person.

There is confusion over what love is. Some identify it with loving feelings, others with doing that which pleases another. It may mean neither. If love means loving even the unlovable, it cannot be based solely on our feelings. If love is beneficial, it cannot always mean doing what the other person desires.

Love means that we care about the other person to the extent that we accept him in his person. What he does may displease us, but he is more than his behavior. When we care about his person, we are less likely to reject him because of his behavior. There will be fewer guilt feelings about rejecting him, and thus less cause for guilt to interfere with a wise expression of our care. With children this wisdom may mean discipline.

Love makes discipline a learning experience. The word *discipline* actually means learning, coming from the same root as the word *disciple*. A disciple is one who follows a teacher—or a master—as Jesus' disciples followed Him. Their life with Him was in itself a discipline.

If discipline is a learning experience, it is obviously a lifelong process. Though its function is primarily the responsibility of parents in the child's developing years, it is transferred to life as a whole as we leave father and mother. Parents, therefore, are preparing their children to live with reality. When you leave father and mother, you take over the job yourself of providing this discipline for your inner child of the past. This is your adulthood, your potential for being a parent, for caring wisely for your firstborn.

CHAPTER 8

A Pattern for Parenthood

After the last chapter you may feel caught in the trap of your own limitations. If it is any comfort to you, I am in the same bind. When we see how complicated we human beings are, it may seem almost impossible to break away from our emotional predispositions. This is because we want not only quick results but perfect results. While the former is unlikely, even a lifetime would not be sufficient for the latter. If you can accept whatever insight you have into your emotional predispositions, you are already on the way. Whenever you can make a constructive decision on the basis of this self-knowledge, you are at work on your parenthood.

Still, you may wish for some tangible, external pattern that you could follow as a help in these decisions. We sense a need for a structure toward which to direct our endeavors. Happily there is such. The Good News, which releases us from self-rejection to make self-improvement possible, is based on a parental relationship with a distinctive pattern. Since God is described as a father, it should be profitable to reflect on His parental approach.

Parental Grace

We have previously described God's initiatory love as a gesture of grace. He loves us with an everlasting, an unconditional, love that provides the basis for personal security. In contrast to our fluctuations, emotionally and otherwise, His love is constant.

The familiar story of divine grace is Jesus' parable of the prodigal son. Imagine having a son who, instead of accepting his responsibilities on the family farm, asked for his share of the family inheritance before his father was dead. Obviously this was disappointing to the father, and he probably said so. But when the son persisted, he acceded to his son's wishes. Assuming he had some understanding of his son, he probably realized that his son might waste the money on "riotous living" – which he did.

After the boy left home, the father heard nothing from him for what must have seemed an interminable period. Then one day the father spotted him – because he was looking for him – coming up the road, tattered and half starved. The father's joy knew no limits. He embraced him warmly, clothed him with clothing befitting the family station, and gave orders to butcher the fatted calf for a homecoming celebration.

There the story does *not* end. There was an older brother who felt like most of us would feel under the circumstances. In contrast to his younger brother, he had stayed on the job. Nor had he asked for his share of the pie before his father was dead. For all his loyalty and decency, what did he get? Nothing! What did his brother receive for his outrageous conduct? A homecoming party! Even worse, the father was insensitive enough to ask him to join in the celebration!

Indignantly he refused. As older siblings often do, he reproached his father for being too easy on the younger brother – much easier than he had been with him, the first-born! The father offered no defense. He simply shared his feelings. "Son, I thought your brother was dead. Now I discover he is alive. How can I help but rejoice?"

The answer was obvious to the father because he *loved* his son. It was not so with the older brother, because his love was conditional, and his brother had failed to meet the conditions. Before the brother's irrefutable logic, there is no answer but grace.

Parental Identification

God does not give His grace apart from His giving of Himself. He identifies with the world of His children as if it were His own. In the person of His Son He became a human being so that He might identify with the human predicament. Through the suffering entailed in this identification, He established His empathy with us. As the Letter to the Hebrews says, "For we have not a high priest who is unable to sympathize with our weaknesses, but one who in every respect has been tempted as we are, yet without sinning." (4:15)

Only through such identification can one really understand how another feels. It is precisely this understanding that preserves the openness of dialog in family relations in the midst of the tensions that threaten it. Did you ever say to your parents, "You just don't understand!" If so, you will know how your child feels if he says it to you. What children appreciate — what we all appreciate — is the assurance that the authority persons under whom we function *understand.* As the American Indians expressed it, Do not judge another until you have walked in his moccasins.

Though God has identified Himself with our predicaments, He still respects our distinctive *identity.* Though He empathizes with our private world *as if* it were His own, it remains *ours* and not *His.* Parental identification with the child does not mean parental takeover. Love does not swallow up the identity of the loved one — or as is commonly stated, mother love is not smother love.

The prodigal son was loved unconditionally; yet he was not spared the suffering consequent to his actions. He took his "bumps." So rough did his lot become that he was reduced to tending swine — most humiliating for an Israelite.

To ease his own hunger pangs, he would have gladly eaten the swine food, but his employer forbade him. Starved in body and degraded in spirit he "came to himself." Swallowing what little pride he had left, he returned home to ask only the role of a hired man.

It was a gesture for help to which his father warmly responded. There was no need for further reprimand—life itself had taken care of that. What he needed was grace and understanding—which the father sensed and provided. God's respect for our individuality is simply His parental appreciation for the uniqueness of each child. Rather than detract from the intimacy between parent and child, this respect for individuality makes intimacy possible. Only in relationships where personal freedom is respected will there be openness and sharing.

The Child's Obligations

The same God who gives also demands. Those who are secure in His grace He calls on to give of themselves. "Freely you have received, freely give." Receiving and giving are functions in a relationship. One is no longer his own when he accepts the love of another. With the suffering love of Christ in mind, St. Paul says: "You are not your own; you were bought with a price." (1 Cor. 6:19-20)

None of us is "his own." Our lives are inextricably linked together in all kinds of interdependencies. We are inescapably obligated to one another. The words "You are not your own" cut through all illusions of detachment and independence.

The obvious example of God's demanding parenthood is in respect to Jesus Himself. "Although He was a son, yet He learned obedience through what He suffered" (Heb. 5:8). These sufferings climaxed in His crucifixion—which He could have avoided. Did He wish to avoid it? In His agony in the Garden of Gethsemane prior to His arrest,

Jesus asked His Father if He could "cop out." Though He had repeatedly warned His disciples that He had come into the world to die, when the time came He Himself was reluctant. We see our own humanity in His as we hear His anguished prayer, "Father, if Thou art willing, remove this cup [of suffering] from Me." (Luke 22:42)

It was a plea that would have tugged at the heartstrings of any parent. He felt sufficiently intimate with His Father to "tell Him like it was." Though a confrontation regarding His mission, the agony in the Garden was also a dialog in which there was free expression. The other side of the conflict also came out. "Nevertheless, not My will, but Thine, be done." He put Himself into His Father's hands—and His Father sent His angels to strengthen Him to carry out His mission. He did not spare His own Son, but rather called on Him to give Himself up for us all.

Identity Through Giving

It is in *giving* that a person establishes his identity. However, he cannot give until he has received. Hence the importance of the parent's prior giving of himself to the child—or God's having *first* loved us. Yet having received, we are obligated to give. Our identity as a person, a unique person, is not established in our *receiving*—from God or parents. Rather the experience of receiving provides the potential for our own self-contribution through which we establish our identity.

Psychiatrist Viktor Frankl says that a human being has a fundamental need for a sense of meaning, of purpose, for his life. In religious terms this means that he needs a sense of calling, of commitment, of vocation. "Nevertheless, not my will, but Thine, be done."

How does one achieve this awareness of purpose, of meaning? How did you achieve it? Some of it undoubtedly has come through your marriage, where you have given of yourself to another. More will come from your parenthood when you give of yourself to your firstborn. Meaning comes through our involvement with people—through our activities, through our creative endeavors—in which we *give* of ourselves. We *need* to give. Though receiving precedes giving, in giving we also receive again. It is the way God made us—in His image. As St. Francis put it in his prayer, "It is in giving that we receive; it is in pardoning that we are pardoned."

As a father with his children God *moves* us, *encourages* us, *exhorts* us to contribute of ourselves, to take responsible action for our neighbor's good. Children also need this encouragement, for they tend for a variety of reasons to hold back—just like adults. There is a certain risk in "putting out." One is never sure how it will be received. The fear of rejection, of misunderstanding, of failure, is foreboding and inhibiting.

In the face of these inherent obstacles to self-contribution, the Letter to the Hebrews says that God disciplines us for our good that we may reflect His image. The writer connects this discipline with God's parental function. "God is treating you as sons; for what son is there whom his father does not discipline? If you are left without discipline, in which all have participated, then you are illegitimate children and not sons. . . . For the moment all discipline seems painful rather than pleasant; later it yields the peaceful fruit or righteousness to those who have been trained by it." (12:7-11)

Discipline—whether exercised upon us by our parents or internalized within us as mature persons—has an integrating purpose. It is goal-directed. To reach a goal means to work toward it. This requires a certain concentration of our energies. It means diverting interests have to be temporarily set aside to exert the effort needed to achieve. The result is satisfaction from our accomplishments.

A sense of identity, of self-worth, is required to develop this kind of discipline. Children by nature want immediate satisfaction. It is difficult for them to work toward long-range goals. The example and encouragement of parents is the assist they need to develop their own disciplinary powers. Adults who lack the inner strength of their own identity may get hung up on the child's need for satisfaction *now* and find it difficult to discipline themselves to achieve that which is not immediate.

The security of your love provides the basis for the positive self-image your child needs in order to work toward his own accomplishments. The encouragement and opportunities you provide for him to contribute to the family and to the world outside help him establish his identity in his own self-giving. A religious atmosphere in which the awareness that "we are not our own" is inherent makes this movement, this discipline, toward self-giving a natural sequence of commitment to God. The realization that we are persons of worth who are called of God plays a large role in overcoming the debilitating effects of the common discouragements. When we persist in spite of obstacles and complete our tasks, we receive the feeling of satisfaction that comes from accomplishment. This in turn adds to our growing awareness of worth and identity.

Two-Way Analogy

When God is compared to a parent, the communication is two-way. Since we come from families, we find it helpful in understanding what God is like to utilize the imagery from this common experience. At the same time the knowledge of God as Father provides us with a structure, a guide, for human parenthood. So we profit from both sides of the analogy.

Though you are soon to be a parent, you are also a child of God, subject to *His* parenthood. This means that the pattern of parenthood we have been describing applies to you as a child as well as a potential parent. Its significance to your parenthood of your firstborn lies in your giving to him what you have received. Through your parenthood, the divine parenthood is communicated. It is communicated in terms of the pattern by which God functions as a parent. This serves as a guide for you as you exercise your own parenthood.

Yet your parenthood communicates more than *pattern* of the divine to your firstborn. As we have previously noted, through the relationship that you will establish with your child, the *relationship* with God as Father is communicated. The pattern not only is a guide for you but is a help in religious understanding for your child.

CHAPTER 9

You Are Also a Mate!

I have been addressing you as a potential parent — which you are. You are also a partner of a potential parent. Perhaps the two of you are reading this book together. At any rate I want to address myself to your partnership in this chapter.

The two of you are anticipating the coming event *together* because you have become partners together in the creative process of new life. Yet you were something other before you became prospective parents. You will also continue to be something besides parents after the event has taken place. You were, are, and will continue to be *mates*.

The Nucleus of the Atom

I have heard Dr. Armin Grams, one of the writers in the Encounter Series, compare a family to an atom. The husband and wife who are also the father and mother form the nucleus of the atom, and the children who emerge from the nucleus compare to the electrons that move around the nucleus — like satellites about a planet. Your nucleus is about to produce its first electron.

You and your mate are not simply two people who have formed a partnership. One of you is male, and the other is female. These differences provide the basis for a specific structure to the nucleus. In the Letter to the Ephesians, St. Paul compares marriage to the relationship between Christ and His church. This is a second family analogy that is used in the Bible for God's relationship to His people. Christ as God-in-human-flesh is comparable to a husband, while the church with whom He is united is compared to a wife.

This marital union as it is compared to the union of Christ and His church is structured with the husband as the head. The reference is to the human body in which there are many organs, of which the head is one. If we were to choose a comparable organ for the wife, it would be the *heart*, since it may represent femininity as the head may represent masculinity. Husband and wife are different — being male and female — and thereby complement each other to make possible a "one flesh" relationship. Although people vary in their characteristics even within their own sex, there are enough similarities to distinguish masculine and feminine trends. The *head* symbolizes masculinity in terms of responsibility, and the *heart* symbolizes femininity in terms of intimacy.

Naturally these qualities overlap between the sexes, and the point is only one of emphasis. The emphasis, however, has its functional significance in marriage. St. Paul sums up this significance by directing the husband as the head to love his wife as Christ loved the church and by directing the wife to respond, as the church to Christ, in giving her husband respect. The self-giving love of the man stimulates the femininity of the woman, and the woman's response in respect stimulates the masculinity of the man. The result is the stabilization of their union as one flesh — the nucleus.

The stability of the nucleus is important for the security of the electrons. The masculine and feminine attraction that makes possible the one-flesh relationship provides the patterns of identity for the developing children. Boys need the image of father to stimulate their own identity as males and the image of mother as the female complement to their masculinity. Girls need the image of mother to stimulate their own identity as females and the image of father as the male complement to their femininity.

Even apart from this masculine and feminine balance, children are dependent on the stability of their parents' relationship for their own survival. During much of the long period in which your child will be developing to maturity, he will be helpless to go it alone. Acutely aware of this helplessness, he will be supersensitive to any threat to the parental relationship on which he feels so dependent. When he knows this relationship is secure, *he* feels secure.

Marriage and Parenthood Inherently Harmonious

Being mates and being parents are meant to go together. Father and mother among other things should be good friends. Your challenge as husband and wife is to keep your mating relationship intact as you become partners in parenthood. The two functions—companionship and parenthood—are the two basic purposes of marriage.

Similarly the role that sex plays in marital intimacy coincides with the role that sex plays in becoming parents. Sex in marital intimacy and sex for procreation are not meant to oppose each other. Yet they can do so. If the fear of conception causes a mate to avoid sexual intimacy or even decreases its enjoyment for the partners, the roles are obviously at cross-purposes. However, we are not merely products of nature but are endowed by the Creator with the potential to "subdue" nature. There are methods of birth control sufficiently reliable to prevent the fear of conception from undermining the enjoyment of sexual intimacy. Undoubtedly you and your mate have discussed this aspect of your married life together with a competent physician or marital counselor and are utilizing the birth control method most suitable to you. If you have not done so, I would suggest that this be an item on your agenda following the arrival of the family scout.

67

Even as the sexual roles in marital companionship and in procreation are not inherently competitive, so also the functions themselves — marital companionship and parenthood — are not inherently competitive. Yet like their sexual counterparts, they can become so. Therefore controls are needed at the functional level also to keep the two functions in a harmonious relationship. Rather than robbing Peter to pay Paul, the controls that promote harmony assist Peter and Paul mutually to support each other.

It is possible for a marital partner — usually the wife — to use parental responsibilities as an excuse for neglecting marital responsibilities. Even as some men use their work as a reason for being unable — too busy, too tired — to function as mates or even as parents, some women may use their children. They feel more comfortable as mothers than as wives. The male counterpart feels more comfortable as a business or professional man than as a husband or father.

Why do people feel uncomfortable in specific roles or functions? Usually it is because they feel inadequate in those functions. Consequently it is not the mark of wisdom for the neglected mate to complain or berate. Adding guilt to inadequacy only compounds the discomfort. If the basic problem is the feeling of inadequacy, the wiser course would be to encourage and commend. When a woman feels her husband appreciates her as a person and as a woman, she will feel more comfortable in the companionship role. When a man believes his wife respects him as a man and appreciates his talents as a father, he is likely to feel more positive toward her and toward the children.

In addition to encouragement, people who feel inadequate need opportunities to get involved. There is no better confidence builder than a good experience. Some opportunities, however, prove too demanding and undermine rather than build confidence. With a little assist from a mate, we can match the opportunity to our capacity. The same positive reinforcement that children need from their parents, husband and wife also need from each other.

Firstborn Changes Things

Upon his arrival your family scout will interrupt the social order of your home. In fact he probably has already done so through the changes brought about by pregnancy. His actual arrival, however, will do a more thorough job of it. He will demand and receive a lot of time from mother. His presence will also occasion the expenditure of much emotional and physical energy.

Most of this expenditure of time and energy will be enjoyable. Some of it may be frustrating: What does he want? Some of it may be worrisome: Is he ill? —should I call the doctor? Mother will require a lot of help, and support, from father in caring for the baby. She needs his assistance with the practical chores of child care. She also needs his supporting presence in the emotional demands that go with being a new mother.

The arrival of the baby will be more than simply the addition of another person to your present twosome. Like the electron with the nucleus, the coming of the firstborn creates a new structure—a new atom. The analogy to the atom is then complete. The nucleus now has something in addition to itself to enrich the intimacy of its internal structure. If your marital union is already strong, your baby will make it even stronger.

The firstborn creates a new and revolutionary change in the perspective of husband and wife. The nucleus becomes the center of a universe comparable in structure to that of the solar system. The comparison is analogous to a sun that precipitates in one way or another a planet to revolve around it. The electron, the planet, the child, are each separate from the structure of the nucleus, the sun, the marriage. The one-flesh union of male and female gives birth to the child but does not give place to him.

Yet if the internal structure of the union is already weakened, the child may be manipulated into entering the nucleus. People who no longer find satisfaction in their marriage may turn to their children as substitutes. The child has not yet developed the personal resources to resist this kind of parental seduction. Once he enters the nucleus, his whole universe is disrupted. The double role of child and mate-substitute proves to be too heavy a burden for him to bear. As a mate-substitute he no longer has the security of knowing that the mother-father tie is intact.

If the child is not part of the one-flesh relationship, he is free to leave father and mother when he grows up. Like an electron that revolves about a nucleus, he can unite with an electron from another atom to form his own nucleus. So the life cycle goes on. Yet if the child has become part of the nucleus as a mate-substitute, how can he leave father and mother to cleave to another without tearing the home apart? Parents who are in this bind put pressure on the child to stay with the family. Even if he is able to free himself, the child does so at the cost of much unnecessary guilt. Also the father and mother who are left behind will have only their shattered ties of husband and wife.

Our age has been called the age of the child. The progression has been from homes dominated by father to homes dominated by mother to homes dominated by children. In our desire to give our children the best, we can give them too much—which can be almost as bad as not enough. There are many tragic instances of child neglect in our day, but there are also tragic instances of children who have *too much*. An overemphasis is something other than an emphasis. Doing *for* a child is not the same as helping a child to do for himself. Parental anxiety is a corruption of parental care.

The population explosion may be a causal factor in this overattention. With so many youngsters in proportion to the rest of the population we can realistically be called a youth culture. This extraordinary focus on children seems to foreshadow a generation gap in adolescence. Over-indulged children are probably to be anticipated in an affluent society. The result of such overindulgence, however, is not satisfied children but discontented children.

The current domination of the family by the child is not good for either the child or the parents. The child perceives his exaggerated importance as a pressure that inhibits him from establishing his own identity. It is making too much of what it is to be *he*. The subtle implication inherent in an overemphasis is that what is expected of him is also exaggerated. These "hidden" obligations stimulate an instinctual resistance over which the child is predisposed to feel guilty. Parents who are preoccupied with their children, on the other hand, may have little emotional energy or creativity left for meeting their own needs as *mates*.

The chances are good that in doing what is best for your marriage, you will be doing what is best also for your child. You are likely to do a better job as a parent if you have occasional diversions from the task. This is particularly pertinent for the mother. Marital companionship is an end in itself. Therefore it needs to be cultivated for its own sake. It can also provide this needed diversion from parenthood functions. You and your mate will need times together—alone. You will, of course, talk about your child during these times—and you should. You will also talk about the house, the bills, the in-laws, and the job. But save time also to talk about things that companions—and lovers—like to talk about.

CHAPTER 10

Your Mate Has His Own Anticipations

We have mentioned previously that you have mental images regarding your firstborn and your parenthood role — images that have developed from your own homelife as a child with parents. Your mate also has ideas about the child and being a parent that stem from his or her background. Since you come from different backgrounds, your mate's anticipations of the parenthood venture are different to some degree from yours. Although we leave father and mother to cleave to a mate, we have soaked up the home atmosphere. It has become indigenous to our own person. We can no more leave it than we can leave ourselves.

Mate's Parental Anticipations
Based on Background

Your mate may have had his problems with his family also, and his mental imagery may show the effect of these conflicts. He too may want to compensate in his own parenthood for his deprivations as a child or duplicate what he has received from his parents. He also may devalue — or even resist — what he has received and overrate what he feels he has not received.

Regardless of how you and your mate may have responded to the distinct features of each of your backgrounds, your anticipations for your firstborn are different. Such differences may not reveal themselves until you find yourselves in the existential situation of rearing the child. The contrast, however, is inevitable. Perhaps your mate's family is more affluent than yours. Perhaps your parents were more permissive than your mate's. His or her home-life may have been orderly and structured, while in your home each person more or less came and went as he pleased. Maybe your mate's parents were somewhat lackadaisical about their children's accomplishments, while your parents were more ambitious in their demands. Whatever the differences, you and your mate have been influenced in one way or another by them.

Rather than being an occasion over which to fight each other, these differences in background call for a marital adjustment. By definition married life is a dynamic process of forming a unit—one flesh—from two different persons. Some wag has said that marriage is where two become one —the only question is *which one.* There are couples who "solve" the adjustment challenge in this way. Yet domination is not the same as union. Both the one who dominates and the one who is dominated are cheating the other and depriving themselves. Their children are also deprived, since they will not receive from the union what potentially it can provide. Though forming the union from *both* partners may mean more "labor and travail," it is infinitely more rewarding.

When the mates allow the differences between them to be expressed, each is provided with an influence that tempers his own extremes. Your mate is the potential balance to your personal traits even as you are the potential balance to his. Each of you can spell off the other when either reaches his limits—particularly in the parenthood role. You have your built-in limitations in regard to emotional endurance and to the perspective within which you view the passing situations. So also has your mate. Your marriage offers each the opportunity to support the other when these limitations are reached. In the normal fluctuations that we all experience, it is a distinct advantage to share the parental responsibility with another, especially one who may see things differently. Marital partners are helpmates to each other also in their parental partnerships.

Assumptions of Superiority and Inferiority

In referring to differences in family background of a particular husband and wife, it is not uncommon for a person to comment, "She (or he) comes from a much better family background than does he (or she)." The 64-dollar question is, What is meant by the word *better?*

There are, of course, tragic situations in families. Should either parent become an alcoholic, the child bears much of the subsequent distress. When parents divorce, their children's base of security is severely shaken. A child who is neglected by his parents for one reason or another suffers in his own self-esteem. Some children have been damaged by the brutality of emotionally disturbed parents.

Short of these tragic situations, however, we may compare family backgrounds on purely arbitrary assumptions. A "cultured" home is supposedly superior to an "uncultured" home. A family with enough money to live in a "good" neighborhood is considered superior to one whose meager income forces them to live in a "poor" neighborhood. Our assumptions of what is superior and what is inferior blind us to reality in both directions. In our changing social patterns we are discovering that the "poor" have something to contribute to the "rich," that the "have-nots" really *have*, and that the "haves" need also to receive from the "have-nots."

Who has the better background? Whose are the superior in-laws? These are the wrong questions. Evaluation needs to take a back seat to observation. Differences in families are as incomparable as differences between people, since they are supplemental rather than oppositional. If differences between persons are potentially positive influences in social interaction, so also are differences in family backgrounds.

The anticipations that your mate has regarding the firstborn and the parenthood role are different at least to some extent from yours. Rather than being a threat to your parenthood partnership, these differences provide a healthy balance. They are a reflection of the fact that your firstborn will have *two* sets of grandparents. This in itself does not predispose your child to an intrafamily conflict. Rather these additional family relationships are for his potential enrichment. So also are the reflections of these differences in grandparents in the differing family anticipations of the parents.

The things that we assume, take for granted without questioning, are often the very things that we *should* question. We bring our assumptions with us from our past. They are often highly prejudiced, conditioned by local color, and basically irrational. They become assumptions because they are never critically examined. In fact we screen out any challenge to them before it even gets close enough to cause discomfort. We assume that the ways to which we have become accustomed are best, unless, of course, they have been forced on us by authorities whom we resent. Any change in viewpoint or difference in functioning is a threat, because it forces us to question our assumptions. Since we function according to these assumptions, any questioning of them is upsetting.

We see this reaction taking place in regard to the changes occurring in our society. Those who are comfortable with our cultural assumptions are disturbed by these changes. On the other hand, those who have been the victims of these assumptions are pushing for more change. Those who are benefiting from the way things are seem reluctant to share these benefits with others. Their resistance to change, however, is not accounted for solely by a reluctance to share. The changes are attacking their basic assumptions regarding what can and cannot happen. Their mental imagery of what constitutes freedom, rights, patriotism, and even decorum is undergoing severe strain. The world they knew is no longer secure, and they are frightened.

Yet change is necessary for progress. The renewal it brings puts new life into old forms and also creates new forms. The old is no longer able to provide what it once did, and becoming rigid and at times even corrupt, it ultimately dies. Out of the death of the old the new comes forth.

The dynamics of family life follow this same pattern. The new is constantly coming into being, first with the marriage, then with the firstborn, followed by his various stages in development. While there is much in the old that is relevant to the new, it should not be transferred lock, stock, and barrel into the new without critical evaluation. The differences in mates, their assumptions and anticipations, provide the stimulus to evaluate. Children do the rest.

Your firstborn will not be simply a receiver; he will also contribute. Providing his own challenge to old assumptions, he will produce his share of the changes in your family life. By this process of change, family life develops and grows. We facilitate the changes by being sufficiently flexible to look at things from points of view other than our own. We hinder the process when we remain rigid in our outlook because our sense of security is tied up with the old. The conflicts and crises of family living put the pressure on these rigidities until, hopefully, they break down. Out of the death of the old, that which is no longer sufficient for current needs, the new may emerge—again and again.

When your mate challenges your assumptions or later

when your child does the same, you may find yourself becoming defensive. If so, what is it that you would be defending? In all probability, it is your system of values. We need such values to function in life; consequently it is disturbing when they are questioned. The willingness to engage in such questioning, despite the discomfort, is what is meant by being flexible.

As necessary as it is to have a set of values, the process by which we arrive at these values belongs not only to our past but also to our present. The *Christian Century* magazine on occasion carries articles by prominent persons concerning how their mind has changed over the years. That such changes take place is not a sign of wishy-washiness but rather the evidence that life is a moving and, hopefully, a growing experience.

The changes that take place often correspond to the stages of life through which we pass. The generation gap is one example of the changes in values that such stages produce. As painful as this gap may be in family relationships, it is not without its positive significance. Since the gap is due to an inevitable clash in life stages, the important factor is that those at either end of the gap maintain their communication with one another. In your case the gap may be between you and your parents or your in-laws. But the time is coming when you will find yourself on the parental side of the gap as your firstborn begins to establish his own set of values.

The social dropouts among today's youth are an example of a breakdown in communication in the generation gap. They are upsetting to the generation of their parents because they are attacking their parents' set of values in more drastic ways than heretofore. In so doing they have contributed their share to the social upheaval of our day.

The fear of change is a manifestation of insecurity rather than security. A rigid defense against any challenge to our values indicates that we have assumed more than we should about these values. There is a difference between knowing one's own mind and having a closed mind, even as there is a difference between being flexible regarding our values and being indecisive. Faith is not the same as prejudice, any more than having convictions is the same as resisting change. "Not that I have already arrived," said St. Paul, "but I press on." We are in the process of *becoming* rather than of *solidification*, and our relationships, especially our intimate relationships, are catalysts in the process.

From the Family to Life in the World

As you and your mate develop this spirit of openness to the differences of the other, it becomes part of the family atmosphere in which the family scout enters. Though it centers in the family relationships, it is a spirit that is readily extended to those outside the family. This is a decided advantage to your child-rearing responsibility since one of your goals as a parent is to equip your child to enter into the world — to leave father and mother. The home should not be a retreat from life even though it can provide a haven for emotional recuperation when the going gets rough.

The spirit of openness will be of particular value to your child in equipping him to live in our kind of world. The so-called American melting pot has never really melted. Instead we are in conflict, often violently so, because of our deep-seated resistance to difference. Our unity as persons is overlooked because of our preoccupation with our disunity at less significant levels. The consequence of such resistance to difference in a pluralistic society is in the stunted growth of the individuals involved.

Yet conflict is a sign of life — in society as well as in the family. The very intensity of our present societal conflicts could be the prelude to growth. If tension is indigenous to movement, we can hope that our current tensions will move us to an appreciation of one another in our differences. As your child internalizes your flexibility in respect to difference, he will be helped to accept differences in others rather than to resist them or to run from them.

The faith by which he reckons with life will be realistic *and* optimistic. Difference is a reality. There are Jews and Gentiles, bond and free, male and female, white and black. Yet through Jesus Christ there is reconciliation. "You are all one in Christ Jesus." This unity in Christ, however, does not bypass the tragedy of disunity. Christ was crucified. But *hope* was not. He rose from the dead. In spite of our conflicts and our tensions, there is hope—and this is *good news.*

You will want to encourage such a faith in your firstborn. It is faith in Christ. It is also faith in one another in the midst of our differences, individuality, and uniqueness.